If I Only Knew . . .

What Would Jesus Do?

**Over 100 Ways to "Walk the Walk"
and "Talk the Talk"**

Joan Hake Robie

STARBURST PUBLISHERS

To schedule Author appearances write: Author Appearances, Starburst Promotions, P.O. Box 4123 Lancaster, Pennsylvania 17604 or call (717) 293-0939

Website: www.starburstpublishers.com

CREDITS:
Cover design by David Marty Design
Text design and composition by John Reinhardt Book Design

Unless otherwise noted, or paraphrased by the author, all Scripture quotations are from the New International Version of The Holy Bible.

"Scripture taken from the HOLY BIBLE: NEW INTERNATIONAL VERSION®. NIV®. Copyright © 1973, 1978, 1984 by International Bible Society. Used by permission of Zondervan Publishing House."

"The "NIV" and "New International Version" trademarks are registered in the United States Patent and Trademark Office by International Bible Society."

To the best of its ability, Starburst Publishers has strived to find the source of all material. If there has been an oversight, please contact us and we will make any correction deemed necessary in future printings. We also declare that to the best of our knowledge all material (quoted or not) contained herein is accurate, and we shall not be held liable for the same.

ISBN: 1-56865-978-4

Printed in the United States of America

What Would Jesus Do . . .

Introduction

When I was asked to write a book with 100 everyday life experiences and how they would fit into the life experiences that our Lord Jesus might have had, I wondered where I would find that many to write about. But once I began the project new ideas came to my mind on an almost daily basis.

It seemed that everywhere I turned I walked into another life experience—such as when the pizza delivery man refused to take the out-of-state check I'd already written even though I'd done it before. "New rules," he said. "We can no longer take out-of-state checks." Upset, I refused the pizza and ended up eating leftovers that evening. What would Jesus do? Not what I did!

He undoubtedly would have smiled and said, "I'll pay you cash."

Whoops. I'd learned a lesson with the pizza experience. Now, everywhere I went the Holy Spirit would prod me with the thought, "Here's one to write about . . . and here's another." Not just my own experiences, but that of many others from all walks of life.

Soon I found myself asking, "What would Jesus do about this?" and "What would Jesus do about that?" I'd wake at night and another thought, one from something I'd heard or seen that day, would pop into my mind—and there was another story.

As you read this book you will "experience" what others have experienced, and hopefully, your heart and mind will grow richer for it.

What Would Jesus Do . . .

When a Prayer Seems to Go Unanswered?

Dear Lord, please save our Daddy!

This was the daily prayer of two little girls who loved their daddy who had a problem; he was an alcoholic. One drink would turn into a week on the bottle—a week that would crush the hearts of his wife and children.

Forty-nine years passed before they would see an answer to their prayers. In the middle of the night, their daddy woke his wife from sleep and said he wanted to take Jesus as his Savior.

Those forty-nine years seemed like a lifetime to his children. With no sign of change in their father, they continued to struggle with the heartache of their lives. Where was God? Why hadn't He answered?

Have you struggled with what seems to be an unanswered prayer?

Meditate on . . .

PSALM 39:12

Hear my prayer, O LORD, listen to my cry for help; be not deaf to my weeping . . .

There's a phrase, "standing in God's Waiting Room," which describes how many of us feel when praying and waiting for answers. Sometimes, God has answered, but we didn't like His answer, so we chose not to hear. Other times, He says, wait on me. We can be assured, however, that He always hears our prayers. We must learn to trust Him with our lives and the plans He has for us. We need to rest in His peace and take comfort.

What Would Jesus Do . . .

When Plans Fall Through?

It was Valentine's Day, but Leah had almost forgotten about it—the reason being that it was during a time when her life was in a turmoil.

Leah's mother, Helen, who had lived alone for many years, was now eighty-six years old and showing signs of physical deterioration. Her eyesight was beginning to fail, and she was having difficulty keeping her house the way she'd done for years. Also, she was having "panic attacks" that would hinder her breathing. This is what alarmed her three daughters the most. For the present, Helen would take turns staying with each daughter for a few days. Today, Helen would go to Leah's house.

What Leah didn't know was that on this Valentine's Day her husband had planned a special evening. The two of them would dress up and go out for dinner at a lovely restaurant.

If you were Ralph, what would you do?

Better yet . . .

PSALM 36:10

Continue your love to those who know you, your righteousness to the upright in heart.

When plans fall through what do you do? Complain and blame someone else for interfering? Or do you accept the situation as it is and move on from there? Ralph could have blamed others for their Valentine's Day gone wrong. Instead he decided to make the best of the situation and honor the choice his wife had made. Isn't this what Jesus would do?

What Would Jesus Do . . .

To Make People Smile?

"Sit down, Susie," instructed the little girl's mother. "Don't bother the people."

Little Susie, who looked to be about two-years-old, sat in the Chinese restaurant booth that was next to the one where my wife and I sat.

"Isn't she cute?" remarked my wife. I smiled in agreement.

Susie's dark eyes sparkled and she wore a big smile as she stood up to look at us.

"I'm Susie," she announced excitedly. "I'm two-and-a-half."

"Hello Susie," we responded.

Again the mother prompted Susie to sit down.

By now, other people, who noticed the little girl, began to chat with one another about how cute she was.

"What a big smile!" said one lady to another (both were now wearing smiles).

Before long the whole room was buzzing in happy conversation.

Have you ever thought about how easy it is to get people to smile?

Think about . . .

PROVERBS 17:22

A cheerful heart is good medicine, but a crushed spirit dries up the bones.

Have you ever noticed how one person in a roomful of people can get everyone talking and smiling? We are to be "light" in the world—let the joy of the Lord shine on your face. It works.

When Parents Push Their Children too Hard?

Sally and Melody, two friends, decided on an afternoon of shopping at the mall. "I need to pick up Tiffany from preschool and give her and Tommy lunch before we go," said Melody. "Fine," agreed Sally, "and I need to feed the twins. Make it about one o'clock. Just call when you're ready."

After hours of being pushed from store to store in their strollers, the four little ones became cranky and sleepy and began to cry. Dragging Tiffany along at an adult pace also took its toll and brought complaints and tears. "I can't keep up with you, Mommy. You walk too fast!"

"We're soon leaving," Melody promised her daughter. But it was another half-hour before the strollers were put into the car and everyone was on their way home.

"I HATE shopping," snapped Tiffany to her mother, "I never want to go shopping again!"

Remember . . .

MATTHEW 7:12

So in everything, do to others what you would have them do to you, for this sums up the Law and the Prophets.

It's quite obvious that Sally and Melody pushed their children beyond their endurance. A whole afternoon of going in and out of stores and fighting the crowds is more than kids should have to take. It's one thing to shop with your kids but quite another to bring your kids along while shopping. Remember to put the needs of others before your own.

About a Bragging Parent?

Braggarts. Nobody likes them because they never cease talking about what is important to them. In life it is impossible to totally avoid them, but even harder when they are your friends who constantly talk about their kid's accomplishments: their son is captain of the basketball team with a full scholarship to Duke, or their daughter just graduated with honors with a degree in chemical engineering.

Whatever the situation, most people don't want to hear it. Not because they don't care about their friends' kids but because that seems to be the main, or only, topic of conversation. When this happens what should you do? Interrupt them and change the subject? Storm out of the room and ruin a friendship? Compete with them and start listing your own child's successes?

Or ask . . .

PROVERBS 15:18

A hot-tempered man stirs up dissension, but a patient man calms a quarrel.

It is natural for parents to be proud of what their children have done. After all they raised them and should take pride in their accomplishments. However, things can go too far, and when pride turns to boasting, things have gone too far.

The best way to handle such a situation is to not explode but to try to quietly switch the subject. Maybe they don't see what they are doing. Or if you think they can handle it approach them about the problem in a kind and gentle way. Who knows, they may thank you for it. After all, most people don't like being a burden to others.

What Would Jesus Do . . .

About Criminals?

It's always exciting when one comes to Christ. Especially when one has previously led a life of violence and crime. Recently a death-row convict announced her new life in Christ and asked that her death sentence be commuted, since she was now forgiven.

Another recent headline expressed the desire of a community to offer immediate forgiveness to a teenager who had opened fire on his peers, killing several.

Jesus is firm on His teaching of forgiveness, but does forgiveness remove the consequences of our actions? Are we reducing the Gospel by accepting a blanket of forgiveness without repentance?

Ponder . . .

Acts 2:38

Peter replied, "Repent and be baptized, every one of you, in the name of Jesus Christ for the forgiveness of your sins. And you will receive the gift of the Holy Spirit.

The purpose of Jesus's sacrificial death was to allow us to enter the gates of heaven. We are always responsible for our choices and are obligated to the consequences. And, as with all of God's promises, we must do our part before He will do His. This means there must be a spirit of repentance before we can be forgiven.

About Aggressive Drivers?

We've all heard horror stories about aggressive drivers on the highways. A wrong comment, gesture, or out-and-out argument between two drivers has sometimes led to serious accidents, fights, and even shooting and death.

What makes drivers aggressive on the highway? Why must they pass every vehicle on the road? What is the personality of an aggressive driver?

Opinions vary about how to handle the aggressive driver. Some say "just let him/her pass you on the road." Others say, "Never shout back and forth with an irate driver." What would you do in this situation?

More importantly . . .

JAMES 1:19

My dear brothers, take note of this: Everyone should be quick to listen, slow to speak and slow to become angry.

Never do battle with an aggressive driver, it will only contribute to the road rage. Let the situation pass. Pray for your own patience and a blessing on the other driver. Remember, the life you save may be your own.

When Someone Lies?

A strong moral foundation is necessary for the good of a country, state, city, and family.

Children aren't born knowing right from wrong. They must be taught values. One of the early lessons they should learn is that it is wrong to lie. To not tell the truth is to hurt others and yourself. When a child steals candy from a candy dish or money from mother's purse and lies about it he needs to know that this is wrong and will be punished for it.

If a parent teaches a child not to lie but the parent tells lies, his/her words become powerless; the child then believes it is OK to lie when it serves his purposes. He also believes that the line between truth and lying is moveable.

A child grows into an adult, and if the lying has not stopped he will lie about adult things—no matter what line of work he has chosen—whether it is ditch-digging or the presidency of a country.

If someone is caught lying . . .

I TIMOTHY 4:1, 2

The Spirit clearly says that in later times some will abandon the faith and follow deceiving spirits and things taught by demons. Such teachings come through hypocritical liars, whose consciences have been seared as with a hot iron.

One of the easiest ways to teach children not to lie, is when they find themselves on the receiving end of a lie. Use the next opportunity of such a situation to talk to your child about how it made them feel. Explain that someone always gets hurt when a lie is told. This is also a great opportunity to discuss the subject of repentance and forgiveness.

To Find Fulfillment in Life?

Many people feel as though they are living life in a rut—working just to make ends meet and lacking time for real living. Statistics say people today actually work more hours per week than we did twenty years ago. So who has time to find fulfillment? If you had the time, what would make you happy?

Mid-life, empty-nest syndrome, or retirement can be a time of additional dissatisfaction. As a result, many turn their lives and the lives of their family upside-down in search of greener grass. In most cases, this does not make them any happier.

Maybe they should consider . . .

PROVERBS 12:14

From the fruit of his lips a man is filled with good things as surely as the work of his hands rewards him.

PSALM 37:4

Delight in the Lord and he will give you the desires of your heart.

One suggestion for finding more satisfaction is to begin to focus on the things we love and the activities we enjoy. Only God can fill the big empty hole in our hearts. He is the only one who can give the water of life that quenches our thirst. But He can also show you a way to seek the desires of your heart and incorporate them into your daily living and work. Trust Him.

To Show Love to Your Child?

"Where are your parents at?" Jeremy asked.

"Gone," Todd replied.

"Man, I wish my parents were away as often as yours are."

It seems that a lot of kids are growing up on their own these days, and it's not just the ones from the "inner city" or ones in a one-parent home. Children of affluent parents are left to fend for themselves simply because the parents don't have time (or don't find time) for them in their busy schedule. It almost appears that the only reason the parents had children was as a status symbol; something they can tell their "club" friends about but never get involved with.

The parents simply throw money at the kids thinking that will appease them instead of taking the time to reach out and get to know them. Telling their children that they are loved is something foreign to today's parents. Perhaps things would be different if they

asked . . .

PSALM 127:3

Sons are a heritage from the LORD, children a reward from him.

If you receive a reward what do you do with it? Throw it away? Or keep it polished and on display? A child should be treated in the same way. Like a trophy she needs to be nurtured and loved; not pawned off on a nanny. Nothing can replace the love of a parent for their child, so parents should make time to be with her no matter how hectic their schedule. The family should be second on life's priority list, right behind God.

What Would Jesus Do . . .

About a Workaholic Husband?

"I get sick of hearing 'you are so blessed,' says Muriel to a friend, 'your husband is always working around the house making improvements: your new kitchen, new bath, and that beautiful chandelier. I wish my husband would be more like that.'"

Muriel continues, " I do appreciate what my husband does, but isn't there more to life than work? Why can't people strike a balance in their lives? To be truthful, I would like to spend a few days at the seashore, especially in Ocean City or Rehoboth Beach. I haven't had a vacation there since before we were married.

"What shall I do? Nag my husband? Pout? Surprise him with a weekend trip to the seashore? (This can be costly. Maybe I should begin saving extra money for a trip.)"

Perhaps Muriel could ask . . .

PSALMS 37:4, 5

Delight yourself in the Lord and he will give you the
desires of your heart.
Commit your way to the Lord; trust in him and he will
do this.

Here we learn that the writer struggled with feelings similar to ours. He, too, felt cheated. But he recognized the necessity for a change in his own attitude. Rather than grumbling and complaining, we should try compliments. Get involved with your spouse's interest, and he/she may be more willing to share in yours.

About a Fender Bender?

After a busy day at work all Scott wanted to do was go home and relax with a good meal, but traffic wasn't letting him do that. It was rush hour and things were tied up worse than usual. He was reflecting on the problems of the day when he almost ran a red light. He slammed on his brakes in time to stop but too quickly for the driver behind him.

"This is just what I need," Scott screamed in his head when he was hit from behind at the intersection. "And I just bought this car too." His temper was quickly rising as he stepped out of the car to inspect the damage. The other driver was also getting out of his car.

Right now Scott has several choices to make before talking to the other driver. But before he does maybe he should

think . . .

Colossians 4:6

Let your conversation be always full of grace, seasoned with salt, so that you may know how to answer everyone.

Whenever we have a bad day, every situation we encounter only seems to pile more fuel on the fire. But we do have a choice. We can either let our situations get the best of us or we can follow Jesus and make the best of all our situations.

With the Best Box of Chocolates?

Three boxes of chocolates—two one-pound boxes with brand names (gifts to us) and one two-pound box of delicious, handmade chocolates made by a small company, located some thirty miles from us, which is owned and operated by an elderly widow.

Which box of candy would we open first? My husband was eager to dive into the handmade chocolates, but I cautioned him to hold off in case we needed to give it to someone for a gift.

Truer words were never spoken, for en route to our Florida house we would be stopping in North Carolina to visit with some friends—two sisters who are always hospitable to us— usually serving a lovely meal and giving us overnight lodging in their beautiful home.

Decision time. Do we give our hostesses a one-pound box of chocolates or the two-pound box of handmade chocolates that we enjoy so much?

There was no debate. Of course we will give the best even though our mouths were watering for the handmade chocolates that we'd driven those thirty miles to purchase.

All we could do was dream about the chocolates and look forward to the kind hospitality of our hostesses in North Carolina.

Always remember . . .

LUKE 15:22

But the father said to his servants, Quick! Bring the best robe and put it on him. Put a ring on his finger and sandals on his feet.

I PETER 4:9

Offer hospitality to one another without grumbling.

Giving from the heart is worth more than any amount of money. This is the best way to show someone that you care. A gift from the heart to a friend close to your heart. Jesus would do the same.

To Make a Happy Child?

Laughs and Tickles, Hugs and Prayers—what a wonderful recipe for a happy child:

- Laughs when the dog runs after his tail
- Tickles from mommy and daddy on Saturday morning
- Hugs all day—every time he needs one
- Prayers throughout the day and at bedtime

When the right amount of ingredients is carefully mixed in—along with the right amount of Bible stories and memorization of Scripture, a child will become a happy child and eventually a happy adult.

I wonder . . .

PROVERBS 15:13

A happy heart makes the face cheerful, but heartache crushes the spirit.

Jesus would agree that these ingredients make a happy child, for he once was a child and understood childish things—like laughs and tickles, hugs and prayers.

With a Person Who Won't Make Decisions?

"Where and when would you like to go for a vacation? The New England States, Cape Cod, the Finger Lakes of New York, or maybe a cross-country trip?" Annette asked her husband, Victor.

"Oh, I don't know . . . we'll talk about it later," he answered. "Do we have the money?"

"But how much later?" questioned Annette, "I've brought up the subject several times before and you say you'd like to go, but you won't make plans."

"You decide where you'd like to go. Then we'll talk about it."

Consider . . .

I Timothy 2:2 (KJV)

. . . that we may lead a quiet and peaceable life in all godliness and honesty.

Sometimes people allow the fear of making a mistake to keep them from making a decision. Perhaps they've faced criticism or even rejection in the past when they have expressed their viewpoint. For others, it may be an underlying concern such as money or time commitment. Then again, maybe they would rather just follow the leader and let someone else take charge.

Ultimately, we need to be able to honestly communicate our feelings. This requires an atmosphere of unconditional love.

About Finding Time?

It's Saturday afternoon and you are catching up on some much needed house cleaning before getting ready for a dinner party at a friend's house. You have left yourself just enough time to put everything away, get dressed, and run out the door when your kids come bursting in from "playing" with mud pies outside.

Your schedule was already tight but now with this unavoidable problem you will have to rush to finish everything and still make it to the party on time. As you think about this you also realize that you will not be back until late, which means you will not be able to clean up the kids' mess until late tonight when you would rather just go to bed.

Why is it that just when you think you are about to catch up with all your chores something like this happens to destroy your plans and send you back to square one?

Maybe you should ask . . .

Philippians 4:13

I can do everything through him who gives me strength.

Yes, we can become frustrated when it appears nothing is going right or Murphy's Law only applies to us, but bear in mind that things are rarely as bad as they appear. And also remember to turn to the One for whom nothing is impossible.

What Would Jesus Do . . .

About Lawbreakers?

Have you ever made the comment, "I don't know how they get away with that!"

Perhaps you were referring to a speeding driver running through a red light, or someone who consistently parks in a handicap zone, or cheats on his income taxes. They may even brag about what they do—thinking that they will never get caught—that their disobedience of the law will never catch up with them . . . but it will.

Maybe these offenders think what they are doing is "cool," or maybe they think it gives them prestige or some kind of power. Maybe they should

think . . .

PSALM 119:34

*Give me understanding, and I will keep your law and
obey it with all my heart.*

Having lawbreakers in society is inevitable, but we should
not look at them with jealousy. Just because they get away
with things doesn't make it right. Eventually, they will have to
pay for their misdeeds unless they seek forgiveness for their
wrongdoing.

In spite of lawbreakers getting away with things, we should
uphold the law even more since that would be the best way to
be a walking example for Christ.

About Facing the Unknown?

"Mr. Johns," said the heart specialist, "your CAT scan and other tests raise some questions. I think we need to look further as to the cause of your physical condition. I recommend we do a heart catheterization."

"Mrs. Connors, your PAP test reveals suspicious cells," said the gynecologist. "I suggest we do a biopsy just to be sure."

How often are we faced with life's unknowns. One day we may feel fine, and the next we may face surgery or other medical procedures. How should we face the unknown?

Think about . . .

WWJD?

Matthew 6:34

Therefore do not worry about tomorrow, for tomorrow will worry about itself. Each day has enough trouble of its own.

Psalm 4:5 (KJV)

Offer the sacrifices of righteousness, and put your trust in the LORD.

Life can be scary and fear can paralyze. The Lord has promised that He will not allow anything to touch us that has not first passed through His hands. He also promises that we will not be tested beyond our ability. There is comfort in knowing that He knows what we are facing, and even more comfort in knowing He is with us.

Pray for His strength and be reminded that He is also the Lord of healing.

About Sex Before Marriage?

"If you think you are going to wear a white wedding gown you are wrong!" said one irate mother to her daughter who was involved in sex before marriage. "I'll spray red paint on your dress if you try to walk down the aisle of the church!"

Sound extreme and cruel? Maybe not. For centuries the white wedding dress has been the symbol of purity—virginity. And in the Bible, God speaks of a *virgin* bride.

In today's society, however, almost nothing is considered pure or sacred. Illicit sex and venereal disease runs rampant. The motto is "live for today."

Is the bride's mother wrong? How would you handle this situation?

Ask yourself . . .

Isaiah 62:5 (KJV)

For as a young man marrieth a virgin, so shall thy sons marry thee: and as the bridegroom rejoiceth over the bride, so shall thy God rejoice over thee.

To threaten to spray red paint on a bride's gown would be extreme. In a spirit of forgiveness, we are reminded that the blood of Christ covers our sins and makes us pure in His eyes. The mother should remind her daughter that a white gown symbolizes purity; then let the daughter make her own decision.

To Mend a Broken Heart?

"Mom and Dad, you won't be hearing from me for a long time," Kevin told his parents at the end of his long-distance phone conversation with them.

"Why?" questioned his mother with disbelief in her voice.

"I can't tell you, that's all," replied Kevin.

Then there was silence and a disconnect in the telephone line. That was over 21 years ago with no word from Kevin since then. Why? No one to knows.

Kevin was never a rebellious child, though through the years he'd seemed to yearn for excitement that lay far from the Nebraska farm where he'd grown up. What kind of excitement? That still remains a mystery.

Every day since Kevin's disappearance his parents have prayed for him and his safe return.

Dwell on . . .

MATTHEW 18:12-14

If a man owns a hundred sheep, and one of them wanders away, will he not leave the ninety-nine . . . and look for the one that wandered off? And if he finds it . . . he is happier about that one sheep than about the ninety-nine that did not wander off. In the same way your father in heaven is not willing that any of these little ones should be lost.

As parents our resources are limited, but our Heavenly Father knows no limits. And as the parable of the lost sheep illustrates, He will not allow one of His own to be lost. Sometimes it is best, although not easiest, to do nothing on our end. The Lord has a plan and we must trust Him, but this does not mean we are to stop praying. We should continually beseech the Lord for help.

About Giving of Yourself?

My sister-in-law, Virginia, is a letter writer—one of the best. Not only is her handwriting beautiful but the content is too (all five or six pages). And she writes a lot of letters to many different people.

This is probably one thing many people wish they had; time to write letters and just give of themselves to the ones they love. But time always seems to stop us from sitting down and sending that letter to our friends or relatives. Just keeping up with our own work seems to rule out the possibility of keeping in frequent contact with those we love who live far away. The only exception is the occasional phone call or Christmas card. When time seems to work against you maybe it is time to

ponder . . .

Proverbs 11:25

*A generous man will prosper; he who refreshes others
will himself be refreshed.*

Giving of ourselves (our time) is what we are talking about
here. Jesus freely gave of His time to others. He was a master
at communication.

Doing simple things can show that you appreciate others.
Dropping them a quick card or note; sending an E-mail message. Think of things you could do to give of yourself to others.

About Biting Off More Than You Can Chew?

I love Thanksgiving—homemade pumpkin pie and candied sweet potatoes—my favorites. Actually, I could make a whole meal of just those two favorites. As a child, I would pile my plate high with both.

When I couldn't finish all the food I had put on my plate, my grandfather would ask, "Are your eyes bigger than your stomach?" Which meant, if you're going to take extra helpings, you should eat them and not waste them.

This seems to be a problem most Americans face because we have been blessed with so much. We have become so involved in what we want that we forget about others and ultimately waste the things we desire.

Ask . . .

JOHN 6:11, 12

Jesus then took the loaves, gave thanks, and distributed to those who were seated as much as they wanted. He did the same with the fish. When they had all had enough to eat, he said to his disciples, "Gather the pieces that are left over. Let nothing be wasted."

My grandfathers' words were a lesson in selflessness. Although they spoke specifically to eating, they applied to all areas of life. Like the young boy in the parable of the "loaves and fish" who, although he only had a few, was willing to let the crowd eat first. And through our Lord's power, that small amount of food was able to satisfy the crowd's hunger without wasting one bite. Would you do the same?

What Would Jesus Do . . .

About a Rebellious Teenager?

She's fifteen, angry, and looking much older than her years.

She's already missed twenty seven days of school this year, and it's only December. Her friends are too old for her age, her hair is not the color she was born with, and her clothes . . . well, let's not discuss her clothes.

Your heart breaks at the sight of her; you know she needs help. Soon, it will be too late, she will be another "failed" statistic.

What can you do?

Try . . .

ISAIAH 30:18

Yet the Lord longs to be gracious to you, he rises to show compassion. For the Lord is a God of justice. Blessed are all who wait for him.

A traumatic childhood or a damaged and warped view of self can often be the reason behind such rebellion. God's view of her through His loving eyes of grace, power, and joy can restore her spirit. We must be His vessel to communicate care and love. We must look beyond the hard exterior and see her fear and pain. Trust God to guide you to help the lost find value in themselves and salvation in Christ.

If a Baby Cried Nonstop?

"A Trip to Hawaii?" our friends remarked. "You're so lucky!"

"Yes," I agreed, "for a long time Charles and I have wanted to go there, especially since I play the marimba, and that musical instrument is so popular on the islands."

Now, here we are on the airplane which is filled to capacity—not an extra seat remaining. And what happens amidst all this hustle and bustle? A baby begins to cry—nonstop! No matter what the mother does to try to settle the baby—a bottle, a diaper change, rocking back and forth and up and down—nothing seems to work. The baby cries all the more.

Think . . .

MARK 10:16

And he took the children in his arms, put his hands on them and blessed them.

Children are extremely sensitive to their mothers emotions. If the mother is upset, so is the little one. A situation like this brings tension, frustration, and embarrassment to the mother. Her escalating emotional state will only signal more hysteria in the baby. Be willing to offer help by consoling and comforting the mother. Often, a stranger's presence can temporarily distract the child to allow the mother to soothe the spirit.

What Would Jesus Do . . .

About a Grieving Family?

"A lovely Christian family," they were called by those who knew the Riders. Two sons and one daughter, all of whom had committed their lives to the Lord and were faithful in church ministry. Then one day it seemed that all chaos broke loose. Mr. Rider had a heart attack and other complications. His body grew weaker and weaker until he became bent over like an old man. In spite of the prayers of those of the church and the family the illness took its toll. Then God took him home.

How does a family endure the loss of a loved one? What can friends do to show their love and support? An arm around the shoulder? A baked meat loaf? Or just being there?

Consider . . .

WWJD?

JOHN 16:22

So with you: Now is your time of grief, but I will see you again and you will rejoice, and no one will take away your joy.

We all know that there is a time to be born and a time to die, but when a loved one dies family and friends go through a time of mourning. The healing process after mourning comes about as friends send cards and flowers as well as pray for the family. Physical expressions of love and concern, such as a hug can be a real comfort. Entrees prepared and delivered in person spare the family from the burden. Also, taking the time to quietly sit by them shows the family that you care.

What Would Jesus Do . . .

With a Speeding Ticket?

"Your driver's license and automobile registration," ordered the police officer as he walked up to the automobile after the police siren had blared it to a stop.

"Was I exceeding the speed limit?" questioned the guilty young man with a fake look of surprise.

"You certainly were," returned the officer as he began to write up the citation, "You were driving 65 in a 55 mph zone."

"I'm sorry, officer, I never noticed that the speed limit changed back to 55. I was in somewhat of a hurry—to see my sick mother. Will you let it go just this once?"

"No," said the officer as he explained the citation, then handed back the license and registration. "Everyone has a 'reason' for speeding." Then, after giving the offender advice about obeying the law, the officer walked away.

Decide . . .

HEBREWS 13:17 (KJV)

Obey them that have the rule over you, and submit yourselves . . .

We're often tempted to talk our way out of situations when caught. Obviously, we shouldn't be speeding but two wrongs don't make a right. Own up to your guilt and accept the consequences of your actions.

When Misunderstood?

Mr. Blanchard is a slim, dark-haired, handsome man with a gentle smile. Being reserved and often quiet, he prefers to be in the background rather than the forefront. Financially well-off, Mr. Blanchard gives generously, and often secretively, to his church. Beyond this, he is willing to do whatever service he is asked, whether it be ushering, serving on a committee, or even cleaning the church if the need arises.

I shall never forget one Sunday morning during the Communion service when a blind man dropped the tray of glass communion cups on the floor. Without blinking an eye, Mr. Blanchard, in his finely tailored black suit, quickly dropped to his knees and began picking up the pieces of broken glass, all the while reassuring the blind man that everything was under control.

Out in the business world Mr. Blanchard is known to some as a shrewd businessman—to the point where he is sometimes misunderstood and people speak ill of him. Things he does for good are thought of as being self-serving or dishonest.

Think about . . .

LUKE 6:27, 28

But I tell you who hear me: Love your enemies, do good to those who hate you, bless those who curse you, pray for those who mistreat you.

To be misunderstood is not easy. We all face that once in a while, but even if that misunderstanding leads to rumors being spread about you, it is no reason to retaliate with the same tactic. Instead, Jesus tells us to love our enemies and pray for them. This is what He did.

What Would Jesus Do . . .

About Common-Law Marriages?

"Hello! I'd like you to meet my fiancé," announced the young lady.

Fiancé, friend, significant-other, roommate. Such are some of the names given to modern-day relationships without the sanctity of marriage.

Since marriage is the foundation for a strong family what should be done about common-law marriages? Should we outlaw them, accept them as an alternative, or better yet,

let's ask . . .

I Corinthians 7:2

But since there is so much immorality, each man should have his own wife, and each woman her own husband.

I Corinthians 7:9

But if they cannot control themselves, they should marry, for it is better to marry than to burn with passion.

It is understandable why two people would want to live together; they want to become more intimate. It is only natural to feel passionate about the person you love, but as Paul says, if this passion cannot be controlled outside of marriage then the couple should marry in order to contain it.

Christians are called to follow God's word by being a light in a dark world, so we should strive to do so in every aspect of our lives.

What Would Jesus Do . . .

About Dye on a Pantsuit?

"I like your pantsuit," said Sally's hairdresser. "Go put on a smock so nothing will get spilled on it."

"Thanks," replied Sally as she walked toward the cabinet where the smocks are kept.

Sally had been pleased when she first saw the short-sleeved, foam green pantsuit with the gold, diamond-shaped buttons across the front of the suit top. It was in a little dress shop near her house.

But today, (a few months later) when Sally got home from the beauty shop everything changed.

"What's that on your pants?" questioned her husband.

"Oh!" shrieked Sally with dismay. "It's hair dye!"

Sally quickly wiped the quarter sized blob off the front of one pant leg. Then, she blotted it with warm soapy water only to discover that the area where the dye had been was beginning to turn white. The color was coming out of the fabric.

After a telephone call to the hairdresser, Sally, not wanting to press the matter too hard, said she would wait for the fabric to dry before she could be sure that the color was coming out of the pantsuit.

Dwell on . . .

Job 12:13 (KJV)

With him is wisdom and strength, he hath counsel and understanding.

Sally was reluctant to press the matter further. She decided that she'd gotten a fair amount of wear out of the pantsuit and, while some things demand action on the part of others, there are times when it's best to let well enough alone.

What Would Jesus Do . . .

About Forgiveness?

"I feel rotten inside," said Sara. "I know I should forgive and forget but what Sue did hurt so much."

"I know that you're hurting inside," replied Mark. "But you need to realize that someday you're going to have to forgive her. It's God's will that we forgive the sins against us."

"I don't think so," Sara cried. "What she did was unforgivable, and the hurt will never go away. How can God expect me to forgive her after what she did?"

Sara should think . . .

Matthew 6:14

For if you forgive men when they sin against you, your heavenly Father will also forgive you.

Even though it seems you will never get over the pain of being sinned against, you can get help. Through the Lord's strength you can learn to forgive that person and eventually forget the whole incident. After all, when our Heavenly Father forgives us He remembers our sin no more. Shouldn't we do the same to those who sin against us?

To Show Love to a Daughter-in-Law?

Surprise her by delivering a home-cooked meal when she and her husband arrive home from work (be sure to find out what night would be suitable).

Compliment her often about her good housekeeping, home-decorating, or other good points.

Tell her how much you appreciate her love and consideration for your son.

Give a thoughtful gift now and then.

Invite them to your house for dinner, or on occasion, take them out to a fine restaurant.

Compliment her on someone from her own family—such as her sister who is adept at computers.

Give her a big hug and mean it!

Celebrate her birthday with a gift and once in a while, a party.

Babysit for her and her husband so the two of them can go out from time-to-time.

Don't criticize her—either to her face or behind her back—especially not to her husband.

Encourage her to visit her folks when possible.

Think about . . .

JOHN 13:35

By this all men will know that you are my disciples, if you love one another.

Showing unconditional love to a daughter-in-law is what Jesus would have us do.

To Know the Will of God?

Life is filled with opportunities and as a result decisions. Often we are tempted to respond to flattering offers. We hear God calling us to a specific ministry, and we are excited. Yet in our excitement, we often neglect to be discerning. Our enthusiasm to serve can cloud our judgement. We jump at the first suggestion of what seems to be a way to fulfill our calling. In fact, it may only be a distraction. Even an opportunity that is good and right may not be God's plan for us.

How can we know God's will in the midst of confusion? How can we be certain we are being led by His spirit and not our own ambitions?

Ponder . . .

HEBREWS 10:36

You need to persevere so that when you have done the will of God, you will receive what he has promised.

Just as Jesus knew the voice of His Father and was in communication with Him, we too can know the voice of our Heavenly Father. Opening our hearts to hear His word as we study the Scriptures is the only way to know if we are following His lead. Trust in God and realize that He has a perfect plan for all of us. He will never lead us astray.

In a Financial Bind?

Buy now, pay later is the way many people in today's society manage their money. Some people cannot resist a bargain whether it is a new pair of slacks or several CD's. After all, not much expense is involved. So to pay later seems reasonable enough. Of course, few people like to admit that the pay later part often comes with headaches over the bills which can include high interest rates for such things as credit cards. Living with the buy now, pay later philosophy will undoubtedly lead to a financial crisis.

Are you in a financial crisis and don't know how to get out? Explore your options, then find the answer in the Word of God.

Also, dwell on . . .

PROVERBS 22:7

The rich rule over the poor, and the borrower is servant to the lender.

ISAIAH 55:2

Why spend money on what is not bread, and your labor on what does not satisfy?

In order to "walk the walk" and "talk the talk" we should be a godly example to those around us. To be known as a spend-thrift and one who continually is in debt and doesn't pay bills on time is to set a poor example to others. It is likely that our Lord would advise us to get out of debt and stay out.

About Being Fair to Our Mate?

"I promised Mom that we'd spend Sunday afternoon with her and Dad," said Tom to his wife, Becky.

"Oh, no," moaned Becky. "Your dad is such a braggart, and your mother is so submissive to him. I can't stand to be around them."

"But they are my parents," argued Tom. "Couldn't we visit with them for a couple of hours? We haven't seen them for three months. You see your parents every week!"

"Oh, all right," agreed Becky reluctantly, "but don't expect me to enjoy it."

Think about . . .

ROMANS 12:10

Be devoted to one another in brotherly love. Honor one another above yourselves.

Tom and Becky's situation is not an unusual one. So often families live half way across the country, making it even more difficult. We need to see things from our mate's perspective and respond with love.

Jesus would instruct both Tom and Becky to do the right thing even if they don't feel like it. We are all capable of being polite and acting with kindness toward others. God's way teaches that emotions are fickle. We are commanded to reach out in love and the feelings of love will follow.

What Would Jesus Do . . .

If He Needed a Computer and Couldn't Afford One?

Dear Lord,

You know how much I need a computer. I've been given an assignment to write this book, but how can I do it efficiently with an old typewriter that doesn't self-correct. It will take so much longer if I have to go that route, and the publisher needs this manuscript finished on time. I ask you, Lord, for your heavenly wisdom to know what steps to take to "find" the computer that you have for me. So, until you bring the computer to me or show me where it is, I will keep this request before you.

Think . . .

MATTHEW 21:22

If you believe, you will receive whatever you ask for in prayer.

God's Word is true. He does provide for all our needs. He may not give us the needed item when we want it, but He will provide it when we need it. We must be patient.

In this case, I asked in His Name and received a computer that is more than adequate to write this and many more books. His Name be praised!

The Author

What Would Jesus Do . . .

To Keep a Good Man Down?

"Don't lift anything too heavy. You don't have to 'sit around,' but just don't do too much—especially until after we do more tests," instructed Dr. Pacino.

Oh sure! This sounds like good advice from the doctor, but we ladies know that our husbands are not going to go home and do nothing—that is, if they are like mine. My husband is likely to go home and dig up the ground to put in fencing.

"Quit babying me," he'll tell me. "I'm not an invalid yet. What's the use of being alive if you can't do anything?"

So what's a wife to do?

Think about . . .

Isaiah 26:3

You will keep in perfect peace him whose mind is stead-fast, because he trusts in you.

If the problem is medical, like in this story, you may have to use a little "tough love" strategy. Let him know how important he is to you, so he understands your motivation is sincere. Enlist the help of friends and relatives. Often times, it is easier to "take our medicine" from someone other than our spouse. Of course, don't leave God out of this, pray that He will make the transition easy. Also, try a new hobby together—use this as an opportunity to grow together.

What Would Jesus Do . . .

About a Telephone Airhead?

You see them standing in public places like fast-food restaurants—the cellular phone locked to one side of their head, while their children wildly run around disturbing other patrons.

They carelessly pass you on the highway with one hand on the wheel and the other holding the phone—all the while their mind is preoccupied with their conversation.

Can you believe there are those who have the audacity to hold telephone conversations while in church or when they are part of an audience during a live television show?

Consider . . .

ROMANS 13:10

Love does no harm to its neighbor. Therefore love is the fulfillment of the law.

JOHN 13:35

By this all men will know that you are my disciples, if you love one another.

While the cellular phone is a great invention, like other things, it has its place. Private telephone conversations in public places can be disturbing to others, and using the cellular phone while driving down a highway could be dangerous. No matter how you use your cellular phone, be respectful and don't disturb those around you.

About Showing Favoritism?

Do you prefer chocolate or vanilla? Red or blue? The mountains or the beach? These trivial choices are easily made in every person's life. It is simple to choose between the things you like and the things you don't like. But what about when you play favorites with the people in your life.

Is it okay for parents to prefer one child over another? What about for a minister to prefer the company of some members of his congregation over others? Or what if a judge likes one lawyer over another? Is there something wrong with this, or is it merely another trivial choice?

Ask yourself . . .

I TIMOTHY 5:21

I charge you, in the sight of God and Christ Jesus and the elect angels, to keep these instructions without partiality, and to do nothing out of favoritism.

It is one thing to have favorites in regards to food, but there are some places where it is completely wrong to have favorites. Examples of this are parents with their children, ministers and their congregation, and judges and those they preside over. In these three examples, problems would quickly arise from favoritism such as jealousy and injustice. The only good place for favoritism is when choosing between doing right and doing wrong.

When the Beat Goes On?

How Great Thou Art with a Rock Drum Beat!?

Can you believe it? But it's true.

After struggling to sing the songs (with a rock drum beat) listed one Sunday morning in the church bulletin, my heart rejoiced when I saw the hymn, *How Great Thou Art*. Unfortunately, this great worship hymn was being sung with a swinging rock beat—with the dull thud of the drums beating down again, and again.

"How can they do this?" I murmured to myself as I stopped trying to sing to the drone of the drum. "I thought music was to soothe the spirit," I whispered to myself, "Oh, God, HELP!"

Think about . . .

PROVERBS 19:11

A man's wisdom gives him patience; it is to his glory to overlook an offense.

While there is a generational difference in church music today, it does not need to be a source of contention. I realize that the "old school" hate to hear their favorite hymns being modified for today's youth, but in the same respect the youth need to be a part of the church. If the "new music" is something they can connect with, maybe it wouldn't be a bad idea to give it a try. Perhaps the church can have two services, one for each type of music. Or maybe they could alternate which type they played each week. In any case, all parties should seek patience and wisdom in the matter so that the situation can be resolved without division.

What Would Jesus Do . . .

About the TV Invasion?

Television brings people into your home that you would never invite!

—Naomi Judd

In the days before television the home was considered to be a safe haven, and for the most part, protected the family from undesirable influences.

But today things have changed. Sex, violence, and occult themes portrayed on the TV screen, whether in daytime or nighttime shows, have infiltrated the home. Consider these statistics from the book *Turmoil In The Toybox II*:

- Over 75% of all prime-time network dramas contain some act of physical, mental, or verbal violence.

- The average child has watched the violent destruction of more than 13,000 persons on TV by the time he is fifteen.

- At the current rates, the average American will view 45,000 murders or attempted murders on television by the age of 21.

Consider . . .

PHILIPPIANS 4:8

Finally brothers, whatever is noble, whatever is right, whatever is pure, whatever is lovely, whatever is admirable—if anything is excellent or praiseworthy—think about such things.

If the television is bringing in things that are impure and unclean, then Christians should avoid those shows. Do not support shows that are in opposition to our faith. Instead, we should strive to support shows that convey morals and things that are pure. As parents, we must make ourselves aware of, and influence, what our children watch.

To Find the Right Church?

Moving to a new community can be a traumatic experience—not only because of all the work involved in the move, but also because everything else is new: the job, house, supermarket, etc. Even a routine trip to the post office becomes more than expected simply because you don't know where it is. One thing, though, should not be taken lightly, and that is the task of finding a new church.

Church is the best place to receive spiritual nourishment and encouragement from other believers. It is also the best place to focus on God. But what is the best way to find the church that is right for you? Do you pick the closest one to your new house? Or maybe you should

consider . . .

PSALMS 32:8

I will instruct you and teach you in the way you should go; I will counsel you and watch over you.

PHILIPPIANS 4:6

Do not be anxious about anything, but in everything, by prayer and petition, with thanksgiving, present your requests to God.

The best thing to do would be to pray about the situation while you attend several different churches in the area. Once you have narrowed it down, keep praying and the Lord will show you the way. You also might ask your old pastor if he knows of any good churches in the area you will be moving to, so you can narrow your search that way.

What Would Jesus Do . . .

About a Know-It-All?

Is there anyone on this earth who at one time or another has not run into a person who is a know-it-all? They never let you get a word in edgewise and are "experts" on everything.

How do you handle a know-it-all? Do you forcibly take the upper hand during a conversation? Do you calmly state your position and then change the subject? Or do you tell them off and then walk away?

Ask yourself . . .

GALATIANS 5:22, 23

But the fruit of the Spirit is love, joy, peace, patience, kindness, goodness, faithfulness, gentleness and self-control.

No matter how difficult or trying a person is, we have an obligation to good behavior. Just as Christ did, we must remember to be kind in spirit. Insecurity is usually the reason for a know-it-all attitude. Encouragement and acceptance can mend an insecure spirit.

What Would Jesus Do . . .

About Cigarette Smoking?

According to the American Cancer Society:
- Teens spend about $962 million a year on cigarettes.
- The greatest increase in tobacco use occurs between the seventh and ninth grades.
- Every day, about 6,000 children try a cigarette and 3,000 become daily smokers.

Although in 1996 an estimated 12 million Americans joined in the *Great American Smoke Out* (an event urging smokers to be smoke-free for at least one day set aside for this purpose) teenagers continue to be the majority of new smokers.

Smoking, however, is not illegal, so what should the Christian do?

Ask yourself . . .

1 Corinthians 6:19

Do you not know that your body is a temple of the Holy Spirit, who is in you, whom you have received from God? You are not your own; you were bought at a price. Therefore honor God with your body.

Zechariah 4:6

. . . "Not by might nor by power, but by my Spirit," says the LORD Almighty.

God wants our body to be His "temple"—healthy, and free of unclean habits. While the *Great American Smoke Out* may work for some people, it will not work for all. Were Jesus asked to comment on breaking the habit of smoking, He would likely respond with the Scriptures given here. Through His power we can break this and other bad habits in our lives.

What Would Jesus Do . . .

About an Abusive Mate?

SLAM! BANG! the chair went flying across the room.

"I thought I taught you how to use that computer! Are you so dumb that you can't learn? I told you how to open up those programs before—now you say you forgot!" yelled Jan's out-of-control husband, Michael.

"But I'm trying to understand. Just show me again," pleaded Jan.

"NO! You figure it out for yourself," roared Michael as he stormed into another room.

Brokenhearted, Jan struggles on in her effort to understand the computer. She knows all too well that this is another one of her husband's outbursts.

Jan and Michael's problem is a scene that is played over and over again in many families—even some who profess to know Christ. What should Jan do about her problem? What about Michael?

Ask yourself . . .

PROVERBS 25:28

*Like a city whose walls are broken down is a man
who lacks self-control.*

We need to realize that an abusive mate can be a husband
or a wife. The abuser enjoys the control that can be had
through violent behavior. In our example here we find that not
only does Michael need psychological help for his out-of-control spirit, he needs spiritual help. Jane needs to study God's
Word, pray for her husband, and be patient while Michael works
toward getting control over his spirit.

What Would Jesus Do . . .

To Be at Rest?

Loud boom boxes blare as youngsters parade down the streets. Car radios are turned to the highest decibels as heavy metal rock causes those in the next car to cover their ears. Violence and news of violence permeates the TV screen and spills out into our streets.

The world knows little of peace and rest. What does it mean to be at rest? We think of it being the absence of work. But is it? Even without boom boxes or loud car radios few of us know how to set our mind and body at rest.

Remember . . .

Psalm 37:7 (KJV)

Rest in the LORD, and wait patiently for him.

Mark 6:31 (KJV)

*And he said unto them, Come ye yourselves apart into
a desert place, and rest a while.*

Jesus often stole away to a private place (the Mount of Olives)
where He could be alone and at peace with the Father. Often He
would pray for the world and intercede on its behalf. Other times
He would just bask in the wonder of the Father.

One definition of rest is *peace of mind and spirit*. To rest
in the spiritual sense is to set aside the thoughts and cares
of this life and open your heart and mind to Christ Jesus.
This is true meditation.

What Would Jesus Do . . .

About a Self-Centered Person?

"How do you like my new dress and shoes? And what do you think of my new blue coat?" Dorothy asked her friend, Jill. "It's designer-made!" she continued.

"They are lovely," responded Jill with some reluctance.

"Look at my hair," squeals Dorothy as she carefully pats her hairdo, "I just had it colored, cut, and styled at the Le Chic Salon. Isn't it gorgeous?"

Dorothy is typical of a person whose need for attention is so great that she is constantly talking about herself. Rarely does she focus on the other person but pulls the conversation back to herself.

Consider . . .

II CORINTHIANS 11:17

In this self-confident boasting I am not talking as the Lord would, but as a fool.

Rather than call her down for her self-centeredness, Jesus would likely remind Dorothy of His love for her, then show her how it is more blessed to give than to receive.

If He Received too Much Change?

"I can't believe it!" a surprised Linda said to her friend Betty, "I had one twenty dollar bill and one ten in my wallet before we stopped at the ice-cream store. I gave the clerk the ten and she gave me change for a twenty!"

"Perhaps it was because they were so busy at the store," reasoned Betty, "all those people wanting ice-cream to cool off on this hot day."

"It's so late, and I really don't feel like going back out," said Linda. "I'm not sure what to do. I have no idea when I'll get back out there."

Linda should ask . . .

JOB 31:6 (KJV)

Let me be weighed in an even balance that God may know mine integrity.

Everyone makes mistakes, but it's learning from them that makes all the difference. As Christians we walk through our lives learning every step of the way. Taking the time to see our mistakes, and having the ability to correct them, not only brings out the honesty in ourselves but in others as well.

What Would Jesus Do . . .

About a Spoiled Child?

"I want that toy!" screamed four-year-old Joey to his mother as they were walking past the toy store in the mall.

"No!" replied his mother emphatically, "that toy is for an older child. Besides, I bought you a toy last week when we went shopping."

"Waaah!" yelled Joey with a louder voice than before. Then he threw himself on the floor and began kicking his feet into the air.

"Oh, all right," consented his mother with despair, "I'll get it for you, but you must behave yourself and get up off the floor and stop that screaming."

Having won the argument, Joey smiled, got up off the floor, and quickly ran to retrieve the toy.

How would you have handled Joey? Would you have stood by your word and not bought him the toy or would you have given in to him? Give the reason for your answer.

Then think . . .

PROVERBS 22:15

*Folly is bound up in the heart of a child, but the rod of
discipline will drive it far from him.*

From little on up children can learn what the word "no"
means. The sooner it is understood (according to the child's
ability), the easier it will be on both parent and child. In
some situations it might just be easier to distract the child
with something else so they forget about the toy. Be sure to
pick the battles you fight with your children.

About an Impolite Sales Clerk?

While walking through one of those "warehouse" super stores, I was searching for their vaunted discounts when I came across several items I could use. Unfortunately, they weren't marked. I tried to get some help from a passing store clerk but she just ignored me and walked on.

I couldn't believe the cold shoulder I had just received but decided to brush it off and look for a service desk. The gentleman behind the desk wasn't any better at service than the girl I had encountered. When I asked him for prices on the items I wanted, he just looked at me and then left to help someone else. He didn't even offer any assistance. I couldn't believe it.

How would you handle this situation? Would you reprimand the clerks? Report them to the manager? Or leave without comment? Before answering,

ask yourself . . .

PROVERBS 11:12

A man who lacks judgment derides his neighbor, but a man of understanding holds his tongue.

We all can recall times we spoke when it would have been better if we'd kept our mouth shut. In the instance of the impolite sales clerk, for the sake of future customers, it may be better to quietly let the manager know of your unfortunate experience, then leave the store. Better still, holding your tongue may be the best way to "walk the walk."

What Would Jesus Do . . .

About Lost Opportunities?

"Mom," asked Tom excitedly as he ran into the house, "Jeff's mother is taking him fishing at the creek up the road. She'd like to know if you and I would like to go along. I'd like to go. Please, Mom?"

Not being one to sit along a creek bank for a whole afternoon, Tom's mother declined. "I have too much to do, Tom." (What she really had to do could have waited until another day.)

"Then can I go?" pleaded Tom.

"OK," she agreed, "but be careful not to get hurt."

Tom went fishing and had a wonderful time, but his mother's guilt would pierce her heart for years to come.

"Why didn't I take Tom and go along with Jeff and his mother?" she asked herself over and over again, "I would have had an opportunity to spend time with Tom. Precious time that never can be reclaimed—a lost opportunity."

Years passed and Tom grew to manhood never realizing how that *lost opportunity* to enjoy an afternoon of fishing with her son had left his mother living with regret.

Ask . . .

PHILIPPIANS 3:13, 14

Brothers, I do not consider myself yet to have taken hold of it. But one thing I do: Forgetting what is behind and straining toward what is ahead, I press on toward the goal to win the prize for which God has called me heavenward in Christ Jesus.

Opportunities lost can never be reclaimed. Remember, every caring mother wants to do her best for her children. And it's the seemingly little things like this that Tom's mom carried with her for many years. The only way for her, or any of us, to get rid of this and other guilt is to confess our failure to the Lord Jesus, ask forgiveness, then put it behind us once and for all. New opportunities lay ahead.

About Humanizing Animals?

"I love my poodle, Angel. She gives me so much joy. She's my best friend since my husband died."

"My husband and I get more pleasure out of our three little dogs than we do our children and grandchildren. The dogs love us unconditionally and don't give us a hassle."

"We don't have time for children, thank you. Our pets are all we need."

While owning a pet can bring companionship and pleasure, it seems that in today's culture some people have taken it a bit too far. They have put the same value on a cat or dog as they do on a child.

Think . . .

Genesis 1:26

Then God said, "Let us make man in our image, in our likeness, and let them rule over the fish of the sea and the birds of the air, over the livestock, over all the earth, and over all the creatures that move along the ground."

Dominion over the animal kingdom does not mean placing them on a plane with human beings, nor does it mean worshipping them. Look at the land of India where animals are worshiped, while people suffer from famine and disease. Remember, the worship of animals is a sin against God.

About Body Piercing?

Tongue piercing, lip piercing, ear piercing, nose piercing . . . what will we pierce next?

In today's society-gone-wild young and old are mutilating their bodies by piercing everything in sight and even things *covered*. It used to be that only "heathen" countries were known to be involved in such practices. Today, it can happen anywhere.

Recently it was reported that in one county of a southern state some police officers visited piercing parlors for the purpose of having their nipples pierced, and in one incident, an officer's tongue—where jewelry was inserted.

What possesses someone to have their body pierced? Is it wrong to do so?

Think about this . . .

Hosea 4:6 (KJV)

My people are destroyed for lack of knowledge.

Leviticus 19:28

Do not cut your bodies for the dead or put tattoo marks on yourselves. I am the LORD.

The Bible speaks against cutting the body for idol (magical or witchcraft) or any unnecessary purposes. It also tells us that we can be destroyed for a lack of knowledge. We can find this knowledge by studying the Word.

About Football Addicts?

Football mania has struck again. These games can eat up all afternoon and evening with other regularly-scheduled TV programs being bumped to another time or canceled altogether.

Anyone can be "addicted" to football. But when you get right down to it, men seem to be the most vulnerable to this frenzy. Some get incensed if their team loses. They may jump out of their seat yelling at the TV. Or, if their team wins, they brag about the victory for weeks.

Wives can be disturbed by their husband's undivided attention to football games. The loud roar of the fans with the sportscaster's voice blaring over it can be unnerving. The wife can either sit in the same room and "suffer through," or go to another room and spend the time in solitude. As an alternative, some wives get together at their favorite coffee or snack bar and talk the afternoon away. This leaves the men and boys to watch the football game without interruption.

Some people, however, do enjoy watching football on TV and are not "addicted" to the game. They can take it or leave it. Can you take football or leave it? Or are you a football addict?

Recall . . .

Philippians 4:5 (KJV)

Let your moderation be known unto all men. . . .

Examine your heart to see if football, baseball, golf, tennis, or whatever you enjoy has become a power over you. If your answer is yes, it is addiction, not moderation, as the Scripture here tells us. Repent of that addiction and ask the Lord to set you free.

What Would Jesus Do . . .

About Money-Changing in the Church?

"I won't be able to go to the religious celebration this holiday," said one young woman, "I can't afford the price of the ticket."

Excuse me! What does the young woman mean? She can't afford a ticket to get into her place of worship?

Since that time (over 25 years ago) things have gotten worse—not better. Houses of worship are frequently holding events that are "ticket only." Churches are run as "businesses" and commercialism is the name of the game.

The free-will offering of the past is now being replaced with the purchase of tickets that may cost up to $12 for certain events with Christian "artists" costing the most.

Are we turning the house of God into a house of merchandise?

It's time we ask . . .

JOHN 2:16

To those who sold doves he said, "Get these out of here! How dare you turn my Father's house into a market!"

If the free-will offering is no longer providing the income needed to host a church event, we should look at the reasons why. One may be that the Christian "artists" are demanding too much for their services. Another may be that the church is trying to raise funds above and beyond the expenses for the event. As in our personal lives, churches also need to find a way to live within their means and recognize that the focus should be to raise our spirits, not to raise money.

What Would Jesus Do . . .

About Walking in Another's Shoes?

There's an old saying that goes something like this, "Don't judge a person until you've walked a mile in their shoes."

Unfortunately, most of us fail to listen to this advice. For example, we may look at those who are rich and think that being rich would solve all our problems. But money cannot buy health, happiness, success, or love.

For example, take a look at the internationally-known Kennedy family. In spite of their fame and fortune, two brothers were assassinated, a sister was born with mental disabilities, and the family has faced broken marriages and other tragedies. (In January, 1998, Michael Kennedy died in a skiing accident in Colorado).

Hollywood's fame and fortune has not bought happiness either. Instead, it has brought broken marriages, common-law living arrangements, and gay and lesbian unions.

Would you like to trade places with another person? Walk in their shoes?

Think about . . .

I Timothy 6:6 (KJV)

But godliness with contentment is great gain.

To look at someone's life from the outside may seem glamourous and exciting, but to look from the inside could be shocking. Don't wish to walk in another's shoes; they wouldn't fit.

Be content in the Lord, for He will provide all your needs.

What Would Jesus Do . . .

About Fear?

In the best-selling book, *Halloween and Satanism*, we read:

> Fear is a debilitating force. It can cause one to lose the proper perspective of life. It can destroy the very life of a person. It can cause both physical and emotional illness. It can cause one to lose faith in God.
>
> In today's society, fear is the entertainment industry's "stock in trade." Most of us are cognizant of the fact that fear plays a leading role in television and theater productions. People want to be "scared to death," and are usually not knowledgeable, or don't care, about the ill-effects that fear, whether in reality or in "fun," has on our health and general well-being.

Ask yourself . . .

I JOHN 4:18

There is no fear in love. But perfect love drives out fear, because fear has to do with punishment. The one who fears is not made perfect in love.

Concerning fear, Jesus would emphasize the need for love. By His own example He revealed how fear cannot exist where there is love. When we "walk the walk" and "talk the talk" we walk in God's love and have no fear.

What Would Jesus Do . . .

About Using One's Gift?

"What a beautiful voice you have," the lady sitting in the row behind Bob Corrigan remarked, "you ought to be in our choir."

"Thank you," he replied.

Bob was visiting Fellowship Church this morning and, as often happens, someone who heard his baritone voice told him how well he sings. It had been years since Bob sang a solo or a duet with his wife Connie. For various reasons they had become inactive in church.

Now Bob was ready to get back at it, and he wanted Connie to do the same. But he was feeling apprehensive. Would his voice be powerful enough—or was it too late?

Think . . .

PROVERBS 17:8 (KJV)

A gift is as a precious stone in the eyes of him that hath it: whithersoever it turneth, it prospereth.

Jesus would encourage Bob to get back to using his gift. He may feel a little rusty at first, but with practice it will get better. Besides, just the joy of singing again can be a blessing. Do you have a gift you are not using? Try taking it down off the shelf and using it for the Lord.

What Would Jesus Do . . .

To Advise the Youth of Today?

If Jesus were on this earth today His voice, as before, would speak words of wisdom for young and old alike. For the youth he would say things like:

Only one life will soon be past,
Only what's done for Christ will last.

Set your affections on heavenly things,
Not on things of this world.

Love and honor your father and mother.

Seek God's choice for your life's mate.

Marry for love—not money.

Prefer others before yourself.

Be content with what you have.

Count your blessings—not your money.

Give unselfishly to others.

If the advice given here is too much for you to follow you can get help by

asking . . .

MATTHEW 6:33

But seek first his kingdom and his righteousness, and all these things will be given to you as well.

Our Lord Jesus Christ understands how difficult it is to follow the advice given here; didn't he take on human form and become tempted to disobey just as we are tempted? To follow the advice given here is very difficult, but with the help of the Lord we can reach this goal.

In a Hospital Waiting Room?

So much of life is uncertain. We don't know what will happen in the next year, the next day, or even the next minute. All our planning and scheduling can be thrown off before we know it. An example of this is our health.

Most people have been in a hospital waiting room at least once which is one too many times for most people's liking. It might have been a friend or loved one we were waiting for, but it is the waiting that hurts the most. Or more accurately, the uncertainty of the situation. Our plans have been destroyed, our friend or relative awaits treatment, and the only thing we can do is wait. It doesn't seem fair. Why can't we control our lives? Why can't we call the shots? Why can't we remember to

think . . .

Psalm 27:14 (KJV)

Wait on the LORD: be of good courage, and he shall strengthen thine heart: wait, I say, on the LORD.

I John 4:16a

And so we know and rely on the love God has for us.

An old saying states, "There are only two certainties in life: death and taxes." While this is true in part, it is not true for the Christian because we know that our Lord is a certainty in our life. Whatever troubles we face, we know that if we turn to Him He will help us. We need only to rely on Him for our strength.

About Lonely Grandparents?

"Retire to Florida? You're so lucky. I sure wish we could!"

Most Florida retirees have heard this said at one time or another. The image people have of these retirees is that all they do is eat, sleep, and have fun. But this is not always true. Some Florida retirees feel left out of the lives of their children and grandchildren. So the old folks retreat to Florida to hide their lonely hearts.

"When we go back home in the spring things do not go well," admitted one grandmother. "Although we stay in our own apartment connected to our son's home, we don't feel welcome."

In this situation it is best to

dwell on . . .

II THESSALONIANS 2:16, 17

May our Lord Jesus Christ himself and God our Father, who loved us and by his grace gave us eternal encouragement and good hope, encourage your hearts and strengthen you in every good deed and word.

Grandparents have a lot to offer their children and grandchildren. They have years of experience in living and loving. By reaching out in love to your children's family, you can be encouraged that good deeds will be rewarded. Remember, building relationships takes time and a spirit of forgiveness goes a long way.

What Would Jesus Do . . .

About a Ministry on Hold?

Tom and Leslie were active in the ministry of their church. Tom sang solos and often had the leading roll in church productions, while Leslie served as assistant to the producer/director. Then, the Minister of Music resigned from the church and moved away. This brought about many changes. A new Minister of Music (who brought in a new group of mostly younger singers and actors) replaced those who had faithfully served the church. Many of the regulars (some being older in age) were now resigned to sitting in the pew.

What were Tom and Leslie to do? Complain to the new Minister of Music? Leave the church and go to another? Or just wait for things to change?

Or ask . . .

ROMANS 12:11

Never be lacking in zeal, but keep your spiritual fervor,
serving the Lord.

To complain to the new Minister of Music would not be appropriate. To leave the church would not solve the problem either; people and situations are the same anywhere you go. Tom and Leslie would be best to hang in and be available to minister as the opportunity presents itself. Getting to know the new Minister of Music wouldn't be a bad idea either.

What Would Jesus Do . . .

About a Child with AIDS

"I won't stand for it!" declared Mrs. Smith. "No child of mine is going to be in a class with someone with AIDS!"

"I agree!" replied Mrs. Boyer. "We parents must get together to stop this!"

Mrs. Smith continued, "I hear they're letting that child with AIDS into our children's fourth grade class when school begins in the fall. Let's call all the parents to unite in opposition to this. Children shouldn't be exposed to this awful disease. Let those with AIDS have their own school!"

What is your opinion? Should the child with AIDS be allowed into the fourth grade with the other children? Explain your answer.

Then ask . . .

I PETER 3:8

Finally, all of you, live in harmony with another; be sympathetic, love as brothers, be compassionate and humble.

Often fear of the unknown is the biggest problem. Becoming more informed about AIDS can go a long way in calming our fears. The last thing we should do is make a difficult situation worse by ostracizing the child from school. Instead, try being compassionate and understanding to the child and the family.

What Would Jesus Do . . .

About Divorce?

The latest statistics indicate that the divorce rate among Christians is now higher than the rest of the world—43%. At first I thought this statistic was representative of couples where one became a Christian after they were married. But that is not the case. In fact, Christian couples are divorcing more than others. To ask why is only part of the problem. And the differing opinions of whether or when divorce is justified could fill volumes. Like it or not, we have a lot of Christians in extreme pain that need to be ministered, loved, and comforted. Instead, it seems, often at their time of greatest need, the church is failing them miserably.

Instead of judging and avoiding them,

maybe you should ask . . .

JEREMIAH 31:13

Then maidens will dance and be glad, young men and old as well. I will turn their mourning into gladness; I will give them comfort and joy instead of sorrow.

Many a divorcée has wished to rather be a widow. At least in widowhood, there is dignity. The widow is lovingly comforted and included in social activities. The divorcée becomes a stranger within her own church, at a time where nothing of her past life seems to fit. The divorcée is alone, scared, confused, and often struggling financially. Like Jesus, we need to extend our hand in comfort, counsel, and love. The pain of betrayal can take several years to heal. Be a minister of God's healing grace and a reminder of His promises of constant care and hope.

What Would Jesus Do . . .

To Help a Stranded Motorist?

"Honey," said Leslie to her husband as they were driving down the highway, "See that couple stopped there at the side of the road. It looks like they're having car trouble and the lady is crippled."

"But, Leslie," warned Randy, "you know how dangerous it is these days to stop and offer help to a stranger. I have you and the baby in the car, and it's almost dark out. Besides, the police patrol the highway so help should come soon."

"Now it's too late to back up," complained Leslie as they continued down the highway. "I don't think we are being our 'brother's keeper.'"

"Maybe so, but I think I've done what is right considering the circumstances."

Think about . . .

PROVERBS 1:5

*Let the wise listen and add to their learning, and let
the discerning get guidance . . .*

While Leslie's heart went out to the couple along the road,
Randy realized that he was responsible for his wife and baby's
safety. In light of this, he decided that it would be best not to
stop. The safe thing to do would be to call for help from their
own car phone or stop at the next opportunity and call for
help. I believe Jesus would agree.

What Would Jesus Do . . .

About a Neighbor Who Steals From You?

Betty and John's new house in the upscale neighborhood was finally built. They watched excitedly as equipment, large rocks, and small trees and plants were brought to the property in preparation for the landscaping.

"Let's put the Japanese Maple tree here with rocks and plants around it," exclaimed Betty. "I can hardly wait until it's done."

"Fine," agreed John.

But Betty and John were about to have a not-too-pleasant surprise, for when they returned to their house a couple of days later they made a startling discovery. All the rocks that the landscaper had delivered to their house had been placed into the landscape of a neighbor.

"I can't believe it!" cried Betty. "What shall we do?"

"I don't know," replied John with tenderness.

What should John and Betty do? Go to the neighbor and ask that they return the rocks? Or say nothing and pray for the neighbor?

Ponder . . .

MARK 11:25

And when you stand praying, if you hold anything against anyone, forgive him, so that your Father in heaven may forgive you your sins.

To steal from a neighbor is hardly the best way to get acquainted. While it always is best to pray about a situation like this, you might also politely ask the neighbor to return the rocks. If the neighbor denies taking the rocks or becomes angry when confronted about it, it would be best to walk away, forgive, and forget.

About Old Folks in a Nursing Home?

"Is my son coming to see me?" a white-haired man in a wheel-chair asked as he wheeled himself toward the nurse's station.

"Not today," replied the nurse in charge, "but we'll let you know if he calls or comes."

"He said he was coming to see me," the man moaned dejectedly as he turned toward the dining room.

It's an hour before dinner and the wheelchairs carrying the elderly begin to line up at the entrance to the dining room. Like infants, they live to eat and sleep. Waiting an hour or more before dinner is no big deal to them. Some just sit and sleep.

But the highlight of any day for these nursing home residents is when their children or grandchildren come for a visit. Living in a nursing home can be very lonely. Some residents rarely get visitors, and they feel forsaken by their loved ones.

Remember . . .

MATTHEW 25:40

. . . I tell you the truth, whatever you did for one of the least of these brothers of mine, you did for me.

Society has certainly changed a lot in the past few generations. The elderly used to be honored by being an integral part of our lives. Now our lives are too busy for even ourselves. If you have a relative or friend in a nursing home, or even if you don't, make an effort to visit regularly. You may even consider establishing a nursing home ministry through your church.

What Would Jesus Do . . .

When Beat Out of a Parking Space?

You and your family are taking a trip across the country. Today's destination is South Dakota with Mt. Rushmore and other sight-seeing opportunities. After miles of travel you have one more obstacle to face. That of finding a parking space in an area where many others have the same objective.

After searching the parking lot over and over, as you are growing weary from the long trip, you finally spot a parking space. Just as you are about to pull the car into the open space, another driver comes speeding toward you and slides past you and into the space.

What do you do in a situation like this? Grumble and groan about it? Tell off the driver of the other car? Look for another parking space while you pray for the other driver?

Or ask . . .

MATTHEW 5:44

But I tell you: Love your enemies and pray for those who persecute you.

ROMANS 12:10

Be devoted to one another in brotherly love. Honor one another above yourselves.

Human nature tells us that if someone steals a parking space from us the first thing to do is tell them off. But Scripture says we should love them and pray for them as if they were our brother or sister. (Also, this is a lot safer than displaying anger.)

About Expectations?

My child, from the time I first laid eyes on you my heart was overcome with your sweet tenderness. I held up your little hands, and as I examined them I admired their strength and form. My thought was that one day you may use these hands to till the soil and grow vegetables and fruits for sustenance.

But as you grew, I began to realize that strong hands and body are only a part of your attributes. You also possessed an intellect that, when developed, would spring forth with a creative mind that would set you apart from your peers. Much to my surprise and delight your years of education would lead you to become not a farmer, but a healer of the body—those hands would become the hands of a surgeon.

Think about . . .

PROVERBS 3:5, 6

Trust in the LORD with all your heart and lean not on your own understanding; in all your ways acknowledge him, and he will make your paths straight.

Parents care about their children and want to see them succeed—the parents often have ideas of what path their child will take in life. However, the path that God has chosen for that child is greater than the parents' expectations.

What Would Jesus Do . . .

If You Were Lost on a Highway?

It was October 25th when Charles and I were driving south on Interstate 83 in two separate vehicles. We were headed for the Autotrain in Virginia that goes to Orlando, Florida with no time to spare. Just before reaching Baltimore, Maryland we exited the highway seeking restrooms. After having followed closely behind Charles for many miles, I suddenly lost track of him—the van he was driving was nowhere in sight.

Panic gripped me as I sought help at the first business I came to. Proprietor Karen let me telephone home, hoping that Charles may have called. No call yet, so my son suggested I go back to the highway and wait in the area where the two vehicles had become separated. Again, Karen came to the rescue by offering to take her car and lead me back to the highway. (Over 45 minutes had now gone by.)

Prayer was answered when I suddenly spotted Charles standing on a street corner. I blared the car horn twice and both Charles and Karen heard it. All of us rejoiced at the meeting, for Charles had been standing on that corner for only 15 minutes.

If you were lost on a highway, think about . . .

PSALM 56:3

When I am afraid, I will trust in you.

ISAIAH 26:3 (KJV)

Thou wilt keep him in perfect peace, whose mind is stayed on thee: because he trusteth in thee.

Even though our body reacts to frightening experiences that we may have in life, if our mind is continually on our Lord we can have perfect peace and know that He will deliver us out of every circumstance.

What Would Jesus Do . . .

It's 11:00 p.m. and Your Husband Drank the Last of the Milk?

It's 11:00 p.m. You and your husband have spent an evening of TV—Dr. Charles Stanley with one of his inspiring messages, and then a look into the life of one who has been "touched by an angel." All the while your husband has been munching on his homemade popcorn and drinking cup after cup of milk.

Later, as you are washing and drying the cups and snack dishes, you suddenly realize that you are out of milk. This means no milk is left for the children's breakfast in the morning.

What do you do? Chew out your husband? Get dressed and go to the store for milk yourself? Send your husband to the store? Or, get up earlier the next morning and go to the store?

Ask yourself . . .

ROMANS 12:10

Be devoted to one another in brotherly love. Honor one another above yourselves.

Remember when you and your husband were dating, how nothing was too difficult to do for each other? Now here's a chance to again prove your love for him. Offer to go for the milk. Maybe he'll surprise you and insist he go instead.

What Would Jesus Do . . .

About an Impolite Diner?

While serving myself soda at the beverage bar of a country buffet, I proceeded to get a glass of water. Suddenly, an arm came by my left ear. Stunned, I realized that a man's hand had shoved a drinking glass past me to the soda dispenser. Then, he nudged me out of the line.

"Excuse me," I said as I retreated to the end of the line to get water. The man didn't say a word but acted as though nothing had happened.

I watched him as he went back to his seat. He sat alone at a table almost hidden by a column in the restaurant. He acted very strange. I asked myself, "What's his problem?"

What would you have done? Ignore him? Tell the manager about him? Or just keep a watchful eye on him and pray for him? Better yet,

imagine . . .

ISAIAH 38:14

. . . I am troubled; O Lord, come to my aid!

I cannot understand what's going on in this man's life. Perhaps he's lost a loved one and his mind is on the grief that he bears. Maybe he's been fired from his job and has children and a wife to support? Whatever the cause for the man's odd behavior, it is my duty, under God, to be kind and pray for him.

When Persecuted for His Faith?

In the world but not of the world; this is how Christians are called to live. Unfortunately, this puts us at odds with the world; we have no problem holding to the fact that life has absolutes. Some actions and life styles are wrong and should not be accepted. But when we speak out on these subjects we feel the scorn of our peers. We are called "Fanatics," "Bible Bangers," or "the Radical Right Wing" to name a few. We are derided for holding to the truths of the Bible and are told to not impose our religion on others; we have no right to, is what our opposition says.

It is not easy to take derision from the world. It is not easy to oppose the seemingly overwhelming flow of opposition to the Christian faith, but should we give up and join them? Run away to our "city on the hill"? Or

dwell on . . .

II TIMOTHY 3:12

In fact, everyone who wants to live a godly life in Christ Jesus will be persecuted.

MATTHEW 5:44

But I tell you: Love your enemies and pray for those who persecute you.

Even though we, as Christians, can expect to be persecuted for Christ's sake, we should not fall to the pressure and away from our Lord. Our goal is not to live an easy luxurious life but to reach others for Christ. This will step on some toes, but if there is a choice between following men and following God, Jesus would never waiver from God's plan. We must strive to do the same no matter what the odds.

When a Friendship Goes Sour?

We met Shirl and Bob in church during a time when the congregation was free to minister one to the other. I felt moved to pray for Shirl and when I put my hand on her shoulder and prayed it seemed that a heavy burden within her was released. This experience bonded us together in friendship.

We (and our husbands) often sat together in church, spoke on the telephone, and spent times of fellowship by going out to a restaurant.

But later, when my husband and I decided that the distance we had to travel to the church made it difficult for us to stay involved, we began to consider a church closer to where we live.

When I told Shirl of our decision I noticed a coldness come over her. Then there was less and less communication between us until my recent telephone message left on Shirl's machine brought no return call. When I asked her why she didn't answer my call, she responded with several excuses, an apology, and the question, "Where are you going to church now?"

The conversation ended with her saying, "We'll have to get together sometime and go out to eat."

"Sure," I replied. "That would be great."

When in doubt keep in mind . . .

PROVERBS 17:17

A friend loves at all times . . .

ECCLESIASTES 3:1

There is a time for everything and a season for every activity under heaven.

Whatever the case may be, I should continue to pray about the situation while sending signals to Shirl that I want to mend the apparently broken relationship. If this doesn't work and the door of our friendship seems to be closed, maybe it would be best to remember Solomon's words and realize that God may have a reason for ending our friendship. I can always keep Shirl in my prayers.

What Would Jesus Do . . .

About Annoying Habits?

Everyone has habits. Such as a morning routine or coffee break at work. Some habits are good because they get a person started for the day or make them more productive, but what about those habits we see in others that we just can't stand? Examples of these habits are all too numerous for our taste: the snorer, sheet stealer, loud chewer, know-it-all, perfume bather, and the list goes on.

Each person reacts differently when presented with a habit that gets under the skin. Some people try to ignore it. Others mock it behind the person's back, and still others may confront (or explode) at the person who has that habit. The only problem is that all too often we forget to

think about . . .

EPHESIANS 4:32 (KJV)

Be ye kind one to another, tenderhearted, forgiving one another, even as God for Christ's sake hath forgiven you.

Through the trials and temptations of this world it is easy to forget about others and focus on ourselves, but sometimes this goes too far. As the above verse states, we should be kind to one another and forgive each other of things like the bad habits we all possess. Next time you come across someone whose habits irk you just remember this verse and pray for patience.

About Daughters-in-Law?

Why does a daughter-in-law often dislike her mother-in-law? One day (perhaps to impress her husband), the daughter-in-law is friendly toward her mother-in-law—but hostile the next.

Holiday time can be most revealing of the daughter-in-law's attitude. While the father-in-law may receive thoughtful personal gifts such as a shirt, the mother-in-law receives what appears to be "last-minute," impersonal or unuseable gifts. (They say it's the *thought* that counts—maybe this *is* the thought!)

Consider . . .

Ruth 1:16

But Ruth replied, "Don't urge me to leave you or to turn back from you. Where you go I will go, and where you stay I will stay. Your people will be my people and your God my God. . . .

Scripture reveals to us the love and respect that should be given the aged—those who have lived longer than us and have experienced more years of life. Rather than "competition," a mother-in-law and daughter-in-law should have a united love for the son and husband as well as love for each other.

About Abusing the Internet?

The Information Super Highway. Supposedly this will put the knowledge of the ages at our fingertips. We can access files on anything from the ancient Far East to this year's NCAA Final Four Tournament. Whatever knowledge we seek can almost certainly be found.

But what if it's not information that is sought? Pornography and pirated software can be easily found and distributed via this "super highway." What can be done about these problem areas of the highway? How do we keep children out of these sites? Can anything be done?

Ask . . .

MARK 9:47

And if your eye causes you to sin, pluck it out. It is better for you to enter the kingdom of God with one eye than to have two eyes and be thrown into hell.

The internet, in and of itself, is not evil, but there are sites where Christians should not go or do business. If these sites become a temptation to us, we should remove them through the use of programs designed to block them. Parents should limit access to only those sites that would be beneficial to their children.

About Giving Gifts?

Husband, do you recall all the nice things you did for your sweetheart when you were dating her?

Nothing was good enough for this *girl-of-your-dreams*. Perhaps it was flowers and a gift for her birthday; a box of chocolates for Valentine's Day; or a beautiful purse for Christmas.

But what happened after she said "I do!" After the honeymoon reality set in, it was easier to pay another bill than to spend it on gifts for each other. The cares of this life took away the *I care* in the relationship.

Consider . . .

EPHESIANS 5:33

However, each one of you also must love his wife as he loves himself, and the wife must respect her husband.

While paying bills is a necessity, it can become an excuse for not thinking of the other person. The giving of gifts to each other is also a necessity, and your spouse should be remembered with a gift—no matter how small. And don't forget that a gift does not always have to be bought in a store. It can be a gift of one's own handiwork, such as a pretty birdhouse that you can hang on the porch, or a hand-knitted sweater. The main thing is to give a tangible expression of your love.

Since Jesus gave expressions of love to others, He also wants a husband and wife to do the same. He would encourage them to remember their wedding vows and rekindle their love for each other.

What Would Jesus Do . . .

About Investing in Eternity?

The recent loss of my brother-in-law, Larry, got me thinking about heaven and laying up treasures there. You could say that Larry's life was, for the most part, ordinary, but one in which he prepared for the next life.

A very conservative man, Larry was kind to his wife and children, and faithful to his church, and employer—not to mention the many others to which he came in contact.

Ten years ago Larry was told he had a life-threatening disease; one in which he would face radiation, chemotherapy, and all that goes with it. But the Lord gave Larry enough time to prepare his family and himself for his home-going. A new room was added to the house where his wife could teach her piano students; their two automobiles were sold and a newer one was bought for his wife; and a digital piano, which is smaller than their original piano, was purchased for his wife to teach on. His last Christmas present to his wife was a warm hooded coat. Larry thought of almost everything—then the Lord took him home.

If you were a member of Larry's family would you be at peace?

Ponder . . .

II Corinthians 4:18

So we fix our eyes not on what is seen, but on what is unseen. For what is seen is temporary, but what is unseen is eternal.

Although it is difficult to lose a loved one, it is possible to find peace in their passing. In this case Larry was able to put things in order before the Lord called him home. Larry made sure his family was taken care of and did his best to prepare them for his departure.

When our Lord was heading toward the cross He did the same thing with His disciples. He prepared them for His death, and although they did not understand what He meant at that time, they did come to a full understanding once the prophecies had been fulfilled.

After the Funeral is Over?

'Til death us do part is the vow taken during the marriage ceremony that few newlyweds take thought of until it becomes a reality, and one spouse is taken in death.

Now is the time of mourning, when the surviving spouse can cry on the arms of relatives and friends. Then everyone goes home and the spouse is alone.

What next? There is a period of mourning which involves a series of steps that may last as long as two years. Feelings such as numbness, despair, depression, along with disorganization, forgetfulness, anxiety, and loss of appetite are some of what the grieving spouse may experience.

How should the spouse deal with these feelings?

Ponder . . .

PSALM 119:76

May your unfailing love be my comfort, according to
your promise to your servant.

Those of us who have gone through similar experiences have been equipped to minister to others. We can be the physical hands and hearts that help the hurting heal. God promises to make all things for our good. What better blessing than to be able to transform your own painful experience into comfort for others. As we witness to God's faithfulness, we testify to His ability to bring them through to love life again.

Just as a loving church body supports those who are in mourning, so Jesus gives love and comfort to them. Our Lord is always by their side. They need only to call upon Him.

When a Child is Being Bullied?

"I don't want to go to school!" cried seven-year-old Andy. "The kids make fun of my ears. They say my ears stick out!"

"Those big boys in my class make fun of my two front teeth," complained ten-year-old Jane to her mother. "They call me 'buck teeth Jane.'"

What adult doesn't remember being a child and having bigger kids mock certain physical features. Some of our deepest emotional scars come early in life and last a whole lifetime.

Think about . . .

PSALM 64:3

They sharpen their tongues like swords and aim their words like deadly arrows.

To help a child through difficult times, a parent can explain that we all have features that are unique to us—some we like; some we don't like; and there are some that can be corrected cosmetically or by certain medical procedures. Most of all we should teach children to accept themselves and others. Jesus loves us all despite whatever physical features we might have. We are made in the image of God.

Living in an Electronic World?

Recently I had the unhappy experience of attempting to reach the customer service department of a large corporation.

Of course, the phone was answered by an electronic voice mail system. The initial recording of directory instructions lasted 2 1/2 minutes, and this was not an 800 number. I then punched in the appropriate extension to discover yet another recording. This one gave a long list of instructions on how to enter the proper codes for my problem. Unfortunately, they did not have a code for my specific problem—tracking down a delivery that was twelve days late. I needed to know *where* my 30,000 pound order of books currently resided! I found my temper rising with each passing second.

At this point, my biggest problem was not their electronic voice mail system but my fear of taking off the head of the next person I came in contact with.

When frustrated . . .

I Peter 4:11

*If anyone speaks, he should do it as one speaking the
very words of God. If anyone serves, he should do it
with the strength God provides, so that in all things
God may be praised through Jesus Christ. . . .*

All of us have been victims of our fast-paced electronic no-
service world. Unfortunately, this can cause us to let loose with
our frustrations on an innocent bystander. Learn to recognize
the symptoms and head them off before you lose control. Take
a breath, or two, while sending an SOS up to the Lord in prayer.
He is the comforter and shepherd of peace—even in our fast-
paced world.

What Would Jesus Do . . .

About Status?

In today's society people are judged according to their status—or wealth. It is not how well you do your job that is important, but rather how you live, what car you drive, and which neighborhood you live in. People are not satisfied with making enough to live on, they want the luxuries of life as well.

One of the catch phrases often heard is "keeping up with the Joneses." We cannot be outdone by our neighbor, so we continue to buy more and more expensive items.

But if we really thought about it . . .

PROVERBS 23:4, 5

Do not wear yourself out to get rich; have the wisdom to show restraint. Cast but a glance at riches, and they are gone, for they will surely sprout wings and fly off to the sky like an eagle.

What is our purpose on earth? Is it to glorify God, or ourselves? We should not get caught up in the things of this world that we forget our purpose as Christians. We are to bring glory to God in all that we do. After all, the best kind of riches are the ones we can take with us to heaven.

To Strengthen the Family?

The family unit (both immediate and extended) is a gift of God. His blessing is on it and it is His delight to see it prosper. This is one reason why He provides a father and mother to give the family a secure foundation.

November 19, 1997 brought an unusual gift from God to a young couple in Iowa. It was a beaming grandfather who, giving thanks to the Lord, made the announcement to the world that his daughter and son-in-law gave birth to septuplets: four boys and three girls.

A team of 40 medical specialists helped with the delivery of the babies. One specialist reported that the mother touched each baby, examining it from head to toe. "It is important that the mother and father *and grandparents* begin their *bonding* with the babies," said the specialist.

Do you think the *bonding* of the babies to the grandparents is important?

Before you answer remember . . .

Isaiah 65:22

. . . For as the days of a tree, so will be the days of my people; my chosen ones will long enjoy the works of their hands.

Isaiah 65:23

They will not toil in vain or bear children doomed to misfortune; for they will be a people blessed by the LORD, they and their descendants with them.

In this century with medical technology advanced as it is, the likelihood of grandparents living to see their grandchildren is greater than ever. To unite (bond) these grandparents with their grandchildren is to invoke a blessing from God on the young family as well as the grandparents.

What Would Jesus Do . . .

To Help a Needy Family?

I often think back to the little old church I attended as a child: one meeting room with a small balcony over one-half of it, a little coat room, and no running water or inside restroom facilities. It was a humble church with parishioners who were poor, mostly factory workers who made little money, but they trusted God to meet their needs.

One mother of a large family, Mrs. Addams, made a lasting impression on my mind. At almost every testimonial meeting, she would rise to her feet and joyously tell that, when their family would be down to the last bit of food and milk, bags of groceries would appear at their front door.

Of course, as a youngster this fascinated me as I wondered where the food came from. Was it a miracle from heaven or from someone in the church? Does God care that much about us?

I wonder . . .

Philippians 4:19

And my God will meet all your needs according to his glorious riches in Christ Jesus.

Most of us believe that our Lord Jesus Christ has the power to send a miracle from heaven to meet the needs of the Addams family or our needs. The Lord can move on the hearts of others whether it be the parishioners, or other townspeople, to place bags of groceries on the door of someone in need. Have you ever experienced this kind of blessing when you were in need? Have you ever given this kind of blessing?

What Would Jesus Do . . .

To Save the Family?

There's never been a time like today, when the home and family are in jeopardy. Both parents might work outside the home, or a single working parent struggles to keep his or her family together. The result is often:

- Latchkey children who come home from school to fend for themselves. Dinner is opening up a can or putting a TV dinner in the microwave.

- Families who rarely eat dinner together or not at all.

- Children who are not taught family values or never darken the door of a church.

- Undisciplined children with no direction in life.

The list goes on with no obvious answers in sight because the answer lies not in the natural but in the spiritual.

Think about . . .

PROVERBS 1:7-9

The fear of the LORD is the beginning of knowledge, but fools despise wisdom and discipline. Listen, my son, to your father's instruction and do not forsake your mother's teaching. They will be a garland to grace your head and a chain to adorn your neck.

Jesus would make the family a high priority. He would have parents adjust their life so that there was time to rear the children with love for the Lord. Remember, children would rather have their parents than material things.

What Would Jesus Do . . .

About Not Sharing the Gospel?

Not long ago I was watching a television show and heard the show host interviewing an actor/orator known for his reciting of Scripture. The host asked the man if he was a believer (in Jesus Christ). After hemming and hawing for a moment he replied, "My faith is private. It is a personal matter. I don't discuss it."

I hope someone will tell this gentleman that one's faith should not and cannot be private. For once we are in Christ we are a *new creature* and are to be disciples of Christ—not hiding the light of the gospel *under a bushel*.

If you, or someone you know, are afraid to share the Gospel make sure to

think about . . .

Romans 1:16

I am not ashamed of the gospel, because it is the power of God for the salvation of everyone who believes: first for the Jew, then for the Gentile.

In order for the power of God to work in our lives, we need to unashamedly share the life-giving message of the Gospel. It is not a *private matter*.

When Justice Seems to Fail?

There is a problem in our society and little seems to be helping it. Presidents and congressmen have thrown money at it with little effect. Talk show hosts chat about it but offer not solutions. This problem is crime. Crime has made some of our cities the most violent ones on the planet, and our justice system seems incapable of dealing with it.

Convicted criminals walk out of jail after a slap on the wrist because the system says the prisons are overcrowded. Criminals walk away from courtrooms as free men because the prosecutor's best evidence was ruled inadmissable due to a technicality. Why does our justice system seem to be failing? Why is she so blind? We seek answers but find none. Instead, we should

seek . . .

LUKE 18:7, 8A

And will not God bring about justice for his chosen ones, who cry out to him day and night? Will he keep putting them off? I tell you, he will see that they get justice, and quickly.

Just because our justice system appears to be in trouble doesn't mean justice won't ultimately be served. It will. As Christians we know this to be true and should be patient as we wait. Of course this doesn't mean we are to sit around and do nothing. Christ calls us to be the light in a dark world, and when the world appears to be getting darker that is when we should be shining brighter. Pray for those in positions of authority that they may act with wisdom, but also work to transform people for Christ.

What Would Jesus Do . . .

About Relapses into Sin?

During President Jimmy Carter's term in office he made a comment about sin that shocked the nation. He admitted to occasionally lusting after someone who was not his wife. People were surprised by this, but it does illustrate a good point. Sin can effect anyone, no matter what their status.

Also, it does not matter how often we attend church or Bible study for spiritual nourishment because we can still fall back into sin. We are part of a fallen world and fallen creatures are not perfect.

The big problem though, is what to do when this happens.

Let's ask . . .

JOHN 3:21

But whoever lives by the truth comes into the light, so that it may be seen plainly that what he has done has been done through God.

Although sin is inevitable in a fallen world, it does not have to be our master. If we strive to live righteous lives in Christ, then we can overcome the world and the sin in it. This is not to say that we will never sin again but that we can overcome it when we do sin by immediately turning back to God and seeking His forgiveness.

What Would Jesus Do . . .

To Give Rest to the Weary?

Countless numbers of people testify to not being able to sleep through the night without having distressful dreams, the effect of which carries over to the next day. Others sleep intermittently throughout the night only to awake exhausted in the morning.

What causes distressful dreams, sleeplessness, and the resulting weariness of mind and body?

Is it the stresses of daily life? Probably so. But what can be done about it?

Ponder . . .

Psalm 62:5

Find rest, O my soul, in God alone; my hope comes from him.

Obviously there are practical things that can be done to promote sleep such as warm milk, a regular schedule, eliminating caffeine, and exercising earlier in the day. But there is also something even more powerful and effective—prayer. Jesus encourages us to accept His rest and peace—not to carry around the stressful burdens of life but to give them to Him. Learn to let go, and let God.

What Would Jesus Do . . .

About Barbie Doll Girls?

"Why can't I wear lipstick and mascara or short skirts?" complained twelve-year-old Carla to her mother.

"Because you are too young for such things—especially mascara . . . and forget about the short skirts. You won't be wearing them," declared her mother.

"Ah, Mom. You're so old-fashioned!"

The pressure to grow-up and be glamorous is all around. Most models in fashion magazines are barely teenagers. Make-up, sultry clothes, and fancy hairdos add to the lure of the selling mystique. Our consumer-led society convinces us that the only way to succeed at life or love is by being thin, sexy, and rich.

How can parents compete with the media and their children's peers to teach good values?

Consider . . .

PROVERBS 22:6

Train a child in the way he should go, and when he is old he will not turn from it.

Instilling a sense of security and a value in dignity are key to raising a child with the integrity and strength to make good choices. Loving your children as Christ loves you by parenting with loving discipline is the first step to succeeding.

What Would Jesus Do . . .

About the Commercialization of Holidays?

Today stores are decorated for Christmas before Thanksgiving is even over. Tinsel, twinkle, toys, and tunes are the focus of our holiday spirit. What to eat? What to wear? and What to buy? seem to be the only questions we ask ourselves anymore.

How can we expect the rest of the world to believe any differently if we're caught up in this frenzy too?

Maybe we should ask . . .

JOHN 5:23

That all may honor the Son just as they honor the Father. He who does not honor the Son does not honor the Father, who sent him.

David Aikman, a columnist for *Charisma* magazine, put it well when he said, "The original meaning of *holiday* in English was *holy day*. A day when God's actions among humans, whether through His Son, as on Easter or Christmas, or through the Holy Spirit, as on Pentecost, was set aside from other days to be remembered and honored."

It would do the world well, if we as Christians would pray for the Lord to help us to change our current pattern, and bring us to a renewed sense of His awesome love with an honoring of His Holy Days.

What Would Jesus Do . . .

About Gossip?

The tabloids are at it again! It's "give the people what they want"! And what they want is gossip. *Juicy gossip* about scandal after scandal.

We are living in an age when people want to know the bad about others rather than the good. Movie and TV Stars, as always, are prime targets of the media headhunters, and now, more than ever, our political leaders are under attack. If there is anything amiss in someone's life, the media is sure to find it and broadcast it all over the world.

Think about . . .

PROVERBS 11:13

A gossip betrays a confidence, but a trustworthy man keeps a secret.

This problem is most obvious in the media where tabloids have "free rein" on the stories they print. But this also carries over to the everyday person on the street. People want to know the scoop about other people. It makes them feel better when someone else has problems worse than their own.

This, however, is not how Christians are to live. If we hear something regarding someone else make it end there. Don't talk about it to others. Keep it to yourself, especially if it is harmful to that person. Christ never went around slandering people. We should do the same.

What Would Jesus Do . . .

About Tree Huggers?

Environmentalists, you can find them everywhere. From shopping malls to our nation's capital. Their collective goal is to save the earth from pollution and endangered animals from extinction. But the best way to accomplish this task is much debated. Is it through more education, government lobbying, or simply destroying factories that emit harmful chemicals? No one seems to know.

In the midst of all this sits the Christian. Fingers scratching his head in puzzlement over what to do. Before going any farther

think about . . .

Genesis 1:28

God blessed them and said to them, "Be fruitful and increase in number; fill the earth and subdue it. Rule over the fish of the sea and the birds of the air and over every living creature that moves on the ground."

Here in Genesis we see God's charge to man to subdue the earth and rule over everything in it, but what exactly does that mean? Can we do what we please and not worry about the consequences? Or are we more like custodians taking care of the place while the master is gone?

While God did give us everything on earth to use for our betterment, we should not waste what He has given us nor destroy the beauty he created. We should be more like custodians and seek to use the land, sea, plants, and animals to improve our lives, not just our wallets.

About Long Distance Care?

Longevity—the gift of living longer has created a new dilemma—caring for aging parents. This is often compounded by the fact that many retirees chose to move to a distant "paradise."

Illness, death, loneliness, and financial burdens are just some of the additional concerns facing today's families. Baby-boomers have become the "sandwich" generation, bearing the responsibility of their parents while still raising their own children. Two-income families, with no time to spare, can find themselves in a crisis with too few answers and too frayed nerves.

How do we find balance and still manage to meet all these needs?

Dwell on . . .

II Chronicles 16:9

For the eyes of the Lord range throughout the earth to strengthen those whose hearts are fully committed to him.

No one person can do it all. Focus on re-evaluating your priorities. A recent survey found that the biggest regret of the baby-boomer generation is not having spent enough time with their parents and siblings. Our mobile society has isolated us. We no longer have the extended family unit to help pick up the pieces.

Consider moving yourself or your parents closer. Learn to ask for and accept help from friends and neighbors. Perhaps even redistributing your budget will allow for hiring help with the house-chores. Take the opportunity to enjoy the company of your loved ones while you can.

What Would Jesus Do . . .

With a Doubting Thomas?

Jesus loves the little children—all the children of the world. They are precious in His sight.

He knew that the hearts of the children were tender and that they would accept Him at His word.

As adults, we have become skeptical with the reality of life. Too many disappointments, betrayals, and lost dreams have brought us to a point of disbelief. We cannot see the light of the Gospel. Instead, we rely on our own strength and struggle to succeed.

As we watch children at play, we wish we too could be children again; carefree and full of faith.

Is it possible?

Think about . . .

MATTHEW 18:3

And he said: "I tell you the truth, unless you change and become like little children, you will never enter the kingdom of heaven."

Renewed faith is the best kind. Finding it can be difficult. Ultimately, it is a choice, a decision to accept God at His word and life as it comes. Accepting your weakness while growing strong in Christ is a key to renewing your faith. Praise and worship via music, drama, dance, reading, or fellowship can take your spirit to the presence of God. It is there that you will begin to feel His mighty presence and find your childlike faith before your Father.

What Would Jesus Do . . .

When You and Your Spouse Can't Agree?

Decision-making. How difficult this can be—especially when you and your spouse can't agree. This state-of-affairs often precipitates an "I'll do it *my* way" attitude on the part of both husband and wife.

How does this attitude of self-will become broken to the point where there is a willingness to sit down and negotiate the problem?

Remember . . .

AMOS 3:3 (KJV)

Can two walk together, except they be agreed?

Jesus would encourage husbands and wives to walk together in agreement, just as the Scripture says. It isn't easy! We must set aside all our differences and then place them in God's hands. Only then are we able to surrender our will. In an atmosphere like this, two willing hearts can flow together into one stream called "agreement."

With Disappointments?

Disappointments are hard to deal with—whether it's something small like not getting into a restaurant because of the waiting list or something large like losing a job. How do we cope with such a wide variety of disappointing events?

It's easy to just get mad and start laying blame. But then the guilt sets in. Later when we think of how we acted we think that God will never forgive us. Should we just shrug off the disappointment or should we hold a grudge? Before reacting hastily

think . . .

JOB 22:21 (KJV)

Acquaint now thyself with him, and be at peace:
thereby good shall come unto thee.

Take some deep breaths. Often we look back at the situation and realize that we overreacted. Everything in life happens for a reason, and God's path for us may not be exactly what we want. Instead of feeling disappointed and cheated, take the time to see if He is trying to tell you something. Trust in Him, for He will never lead you astray.

When Cheated in a Business Deal?

Colonel Harland Sanders of *Kentucky Fried Chicken* fame had many business dealings throughout his long life. In those days a handshake usually was enough for two people to make an agreement. That suited the Colonel just fine, "except for one time when a man took me across in a soft ice-cream deal. I paid it no mind, and the man was out of business in just a year."

Have you ever been cheated in a business deal? Here Colonel Sanders got taken by a man dealing in ice-cream. He obviously lost money on the deal, but what was his reaction to it all? Did he get angry and try to get even, or did he

ponder . . .

ROMANS 12:19

Do not take revenge, my friends, but leave room for God's wrath, for it is written: "It is mine to avenge; I will repay," says the Lord.

While we may feel like retaliating on someone who has cheated us, our Lord says it is not our place to do so. Maybe we should recall what the Colonel did. He didn't let that setback stop him from continuing on, and eventually he founded a famous restaurant chain. I think the Lord would want us to do the same; forget about revenge and persevere toward our goals.

About Worry?

Some of us only worry over "big" things like losing our job, or health-related situations. Yet many worry over almost everything like: making a presentation even though you've been prepared for weeks, what will happen next week, what will happen next year. Worry can become so controlling that it not only paralyzes us, but it takes all the joy out of life.

Regardless of which type of "worrying" you do, is it what God wants us to do?

Stop and ask . . .

Luke 12:25, 26

Who of you by worrying can add a single hour to his life? Since you cannot do this very little thing, why do you worry about the rest?

It's one thing to have conscientious concern about something. Thinking it through and considering the options available to us is helpful in dealing with difficult or stressful times. As the verse says, worrying will not add a single hour to your life. Nor will it add a penny to your pocket. Don't let Satan use worry as a weapon against you. Trust that God has a plan and will provide all our needs whether it's a new job or strength for a presentation. He will not fail us.

To Tell Me I'm His?

"How can I know that I'm a Christian?" Cindy asked Josh, her counselor, at the conclusion of the church youth rally. "I was baptized when I was a baby. Isn't that enough?"

"No," replied Josh. "Becoming a Christian isn't something that anyone can do for you (such as infant baptism); it's a decision that you have to make—to confess your sins to God and ask His forgiveness. Then, turn away from any known sins. You will want to find Christian friends who will help you begin your new life in Christ. Read this Bible each day and it will teach you how to live the Christian life. Begin reading here—where I put the bookmark."

"But how will I know for sure?"

Consider . . .